LETTERS TO A LOVELY LADY

RICKEY WILLIAMS II

CONTENTS

R. Williams & Associate, LLC
P.O. Box 346
Marietta, GA 30061

Library of Congress Cataloging-in-Publication Data

ISBN: 978-0-692-19429-4
LCCN: 2018911062

www.rwilliamsii.com
Email info@rwilliamsii.com to book Rickey Williams II for your speaking engagement
Social Media: @r.williamsii
Rickey Williams II,
Letters To A Lovely Lady
Published by: R. Williams & Associate, LLC: P.O. Box 346 Marietta, GA 30061

*T*o This Special Lovely Lady

WHILE REMINISCING over the accumulated years of my life, I recognize the best love I've ever felt came while in your arms. The arms of another man's wife. There is just something about your touch that possesses the ability to take away every care of my world. Your words have the ability to calm the stormy sea of my soul. Wisdom flows when you speak, and womanhood when you walk. You are a pillar in your community. With a heart of gold, the love that you give is valued far beyond diamonds. All I can say is, thank you Mama.

WITH THE DEEPEST LOVE,
    Your Son

*D*ear Lovely Lady,

PLEASE UNDERSTAND what I'm getting ready to tell you. It's imperative that you grasp this concept. You must be complete within yourself before you can engage the man molded by God himself just for you. Isn't it just an overwhelming feeling to know that out of over seven billion people in this world, one was made just for you? That should be enough motivation right there to get yourself together. You don't want to miss out on him because you didn't prep like you should have. One of the worst scenarios would be if you actually get him; in his arms in his heart. You'd be the one he leaves work early for. The one he holds as his world, not just his girl. But you really weren't ready for him because you were at 98%. As a result, you lose him. Lovely lady, you have to be 100% complete.

WITH LOVE,
    A Helpful Heart

*D*ear Lovely Lady,

YOUR FEMININITY IS YOUR MASCULINITY. When the term masculinity is used, it refers to strength. Typically, the strength of a man. Today, I want you to consider masculinity from the viewpoint of being strong, period. You are strong because you are a woman. The softness of your voice has the ability to bring peace where there is chaos. The gentleness in your touch transfers positive energy to whatever you place your hand to. Your ability to bring forth life is the essence of your strength. But even if by some reason you cannot, know that you are no less of a woman. Gracefulness covers the land you walk upon. You are strong. You are a woman.

SINCERELY,
    A Strong Man

*D*ear Lovely Lady,

YOU ARE BEING ATTACKED because you are getting ready to walk into greatness. That vision you have is about to manifest itself. Rest in the fact that the battle is going to work in your favor if you just keep pushing forward. So go put on your high heels and walk through the battlefield.

SINCERELY,
    Your Protector

A Lane of Virtue

There's power in her prayers which means
there's power in her words,
A woman who stands in the gap for those
she loves and the world,
Her heart is as precious and beautiful as a pearl,
I wonder if she knew how special she'd be
when she was just a little girl,
The fragrance of her virtue fills whatever room she inhabits,
Habits of no compromise make her temple a palace,
Kings reside in palaces but in her house, only one,
The King of Kings and Lord and Lords, He calls her home,
He protects His domicile,
Guarding her heart from any man who's actually a child,
A priceless work of art is what she is,
My prayer is God keeps blessing her day out and day in.

*D*ear Lovely Lady,

THERE IS a reason that you should never refer to yourself as a female. Always call yourself a woman. Why? A female is a generic term to describe a gender. There's nothing generic or common about you. When you say woman, certain characteristics are automatically conferred upon you. Think about it. When have you ever heard of someone referring to a Bentley as just a car? No. It's called, "A Bentley." Saying the name Bentley puts you in another frame of mind where there is no need to use any other words to tell how great of a vehicle it is; as with the word "woman." It encompasses all of the beautiful adjectives that I can use to describe how valuable you are. Instead of calling you wise, virtuous, compassionate, ambitious, affectionate, so on and so forth. I just call you a woman. From this day forward, you shall refer to yourself as a Woman.

YOURS TRULY,
   A Man

*D*ear Lovely Lady,

THIS DAY WAS NOT MEANT to destroy you. It was brought to grow you. There is another level you have to ascend to. The only way in which you can get there is if you have obtained the growth this level requires. Be fearless and faithful. Don't give up and don't give in. I urge you, get your growth out of the pain.

WITH RESPECT,
   Your Support System

*D*ear Lovely Lady,

I WANT you to smile no matter what. There's someone who needs your smile today. You may not know who it is, but they will not make it if you don't smile. Put your smile on, go to the mirror and look at your smile. Guess what? You will make it because you smiled!

SINCERELY,
     Your Smile Giver

*D*ear Lovely Lady,

As you allow the tears to fall from your eyes, know it's okay. Don't worry about the situation, that's just temporary. There's an everlasting effect from your tears. See your tears are the water from which the seeds that you're sewing right now shall grow. Rest assured once you are done crying, your soul will feel cleansed. When the day comes that you harvest the seeds you've sewn, guess what? Your tears will have paid off for you.

Sincerely,
    Your Tear Catcher

Last Tear

The last tear, the most powerful drop of water I know of,
Though there are others like it,
The problem is they weren't the last one,
They only spoke to the fact that I was
still in the midst of pain,
But when I could no longer cry,
My last tear said here I am,
In that last tear is freedom,
In that last tear is cleansing,
In that last tear is a release of my soul,
Crying my last tear meant the ending of my hurt,
Crying my last tear meant I wasn't
taking anymore nonsense,
Crying my last tear was the beginning
of a new chapter in my life,
Crying my last tear meant no more strongholds
from that which has weighed me down,
Crying my last tear meant that now I could love me.

*D*ear Lovely Lady,

TODAY WILL you do me a favor? Go to another woman and speak life to her. Tell her that she is beautiful. She is smart. She is talented. She has worth. She has value. Let her know she is not alone. Tell her that you stand with her. Why do I want you to do this? It's your duty as a woman to encourage your fellow woman. Also because you are beautiful. You are smart. You are talented. You have worth. You have value. You are not alone. I stand with you.

SINCERELY,
    Your Support System

*D*ear Lovely Lady,

YOU HAVE NOT COME this far to stop now. I know you're tired. As strong as you are, there's no reason you can't follow through. The future you is depending on the present you. Don't tell yourself you can make it. Tell yourself you have made it. Speak to your expectations not to your situation.

YOURS TRULY,
    Your Personal Motivator

*D*ear Lovely Lady,

AFTER READING your heart's story, all I can say is, to God be the glory. All of the things that you endured threatened to take you down, but when I look you're still standing. I have good news and bad news for you. The bad news is, you have more heart wrenching experiences to go through. The good news is, you are going to be stronger than you are now. In life, we can get to a point after we have been through a lot, where we think we are finished going through. There's always a test waiting on you. Why? Your elevation will never stop. Your future needs you to endure.

SINCERELY,
Your Forewarning

*D*ear Lovely Lady,

AS I CRAFTED EACH STROKE, of each letter, of each word, of every paragraph, I want you to know it was with the thought of you, encompassing my mind, massaging my heart, manipulating every stroke. Strong is the thought of you. But even stronger is my love for you.

WITH LOVE,
   A Man Who Loves You Unconditionally

*D*ear Lovely Lady,

I FIND it selfish for me to ask you to take me as I am. I'm broken and it's not your job to fix my heart. Rest in the fact that broken things can be fixed. As I place the pieces back together, I look forward to the day I make you my happily ever after. If there happens to be another who captures your heart before I can rebuild, my prayer is that your heart resides in a house that will never fall.

SINCERELY,
   A Lover's Humble Heart

Giving Souls

I met a genuine soul, but my soul wasn't genuine,
I tainted hers and she gave me a healing,
Humility I learned, ambition got firm,
A friend like I'd never met,
A drive where the limit wasn't set,
Now here's a soul smeared with filth,
Unknowingly I delivered it like a gift,
So when I sit and reminisce,
Everything I received were actions I committed
But my memory tried to dismiss,
My prayer is that her soul regains and exceeds that initial value,
Well, as for me, I'm getting better.

*D*ear Lovely Lady,

THERE IS no such thing as one more time. I don't have one more chance to get this right. In believing I have no more chances, I have come to the realization that this is my last opportunity. I have to step up now. Not next month, not next week, not tomorrow. There is no better time than now.

YOURS TRULY,
  Mr. Right Now

$\mathcal{D}$ear Lovely Lady,

As I watch the heart I love, love another, I find myself grieving and celebrating simultaneously. Two terms that are mutually exclusive. See as I grieve the loss of your love, I'm elated you have found a love to house your heart. My grief is a result of my own afflictions. When I was given the honor of holding your heart, I hurt it. One thing I know for sure is if our paths were to ever align once more, these hands will be ready to receive.

Sincerely,
　Happy Hurt Heart

The Lost Love

I remember the day I lost your love,
I was dismissed from your heart,
This had to be a dream,
Surely I'd wake up.
Then all of a sudden you were my lady again,
Back in my arms,
But that's when I realized it was a dream,
The reality was what I thought to be the dream, and what I
thought to be a dream the reality.
Will I ever have you back?
Only God knows.

*D*ear Lovely Lady,

TO THE LOVE I've never met, I want you to know that I'm thinking about you. As I travel through this thing called life, I'm positioning myself for our encounter. Everyday, I'm molding myself more and more into the man who you need by your side. The man who takes an active role in your dreams and ambitions. I plead with you to ensure you are ready too. While reading this, know this is your positioning time also. You may have had some situations that didn't work out for you, but don't allow them to make you bitter. Baby you can only get better.

SINCERELY,
   Your Future BEST FRIEND

Hooked

In the midst of an angry sea
Two fishermen ask one another, *What do you see?*
As they marvel at the site,
One fishermen's lines becomes tight.
Exactly where they're taking a look is where something
was on the hook.
Immediately, there was a break in the surface,
A revelation on purpose,
Only once had the fisher seen a species of this kind,
So he asked the other fisherman,
What do you do when love is on the line?

*D*ear Lovely Lady,

"WHAT ARE YOUR INTENTIONS WITH ME?" That's the question you asked me. Silence... I glimpsed at your face to behold your joyful expression to have a linear relationship with time at a negative slope. As time drew on, the more disheartened you appeared. How am I to place in words these deep feelings for you? Can I say that my intentions are good? No, that's not good enough. Be specific. My intentions are to grow with you. Mentally we will grow by reading together. After we read, we'll discuss the nuances of our interpretations. Or let's take a trip to the museum. There we can stimulate our brains' occipital lobes. How about we ride and listen to the message in the music. Either way, I want to invigorate two beautiful minds. Your spirit... that's what's most important to me. My intent is to speak to your soul, but not directly. See God is the link. In order for me to get to your soul, I have to go through Him. So when I pray, I include you. I ask Him for the knowledge and the wisdom to guide you according to his will. I pray that He allows your good days to outweigh your bad days. And when you do have a bad day, to give me the words or lack thereof to help you make it through. I pray that you always see beauty in a world full of beasts. I pray that He allows you to keep your wings since you're my angel watching over me.

SINCERELY,
My Intentions For You

*D*ear Lovely Lady,

As I THINK ABOUT YOU, all of the characteristics that make you come rushing into my mind. This specific grouping of characteristics places you in a class of your own. No other woman in this world can compare to you. You are uniquely you. That's why you are so special. Every day you get up, I want you to remember that.

KIND REGARDS,
   Your Unique Identifier

*D*ear Lovely Lady,

SOMETIMES I WISH you could see you through my eyes. Every positive, and even every blemish. When I gaze upon you I can't help but think what did the world do so right that we deserve to be graced with your presence. This is not to make you become arrogant; but, I was always taught to give credit where credit is due. Ms. Lady, credit is due to you.

SINCERELY,
    Your Credit Giver

*D*ear Lovely Lady,

I WANT you to always work on becoming a better you. Realize there may be some validity in what someone says about you. Never mind their delivery, just get your advancement from it. Keep in mind this is not being said for you to constantly worry about others' thoughts of you. Be you, live for you, become the best you, and everything that's meant for you will come to you.

SINCERELY,
    The Man Who Sees the Best You

*D*ear Lovely Lady,

EVERY DAY WILL HAVE its challenges with us. We have to stick it out. They will pass, believe me. I don't want to pass up the opportunity to get back right with you. The last thing I want to see is you in the arms of another. So my pride is out of the window never to return. All I want to do is love you.

SINCERELY,
    Your Love For Life

The Army of Us

I'd rather you fight for me than fight with me,
Everything is not your fault, there are parts I contribute too,
Let's put down our swords and let me put up our shield,
To protect us from the world of superficial,
Officially super is how I see you as a woman,
Waging war with a wild world,
We win.

*D*ear Lovely Lady,

WHEN WE FIRST MET, you asked me how many times had I been in love and I gave you an answer. Now I have a confession. Since we have entered into the covenant relationship that number has increased. If I only think about the past year, I can honestly say I've fallen in love 365 times. Each morning when I wake up, I fall in love with you all over again. With each 24 hours God allows me to share a life with your beautiful spirit, my love for you not only grows, it resets. What I love about the resetting of my love is the daily freshness. When I open my eyes to behold the beauty of a face crafted by the hands of God himself, no greater feeling arrests my heart. The only thing I can do is drop to my knees and pray a prayer of thanks for you.

WITH LOVE,
The Man Who Falls in Love With You Daily

Heart of Art

When my heart experiences any emotion,
That's when pen and paper gets put into motion,
Your heart feels something every day,
Every 24 you have something to say,
Document your heart,
Let your documentation serve as a
beautiful work of art,
Let this pen be the instrument,
Each stroke a lovely sentiment,
I want to read your smile,
Place it in a file,
Interpret any tears,
Erase any fears.

*D*ear Lovely Lady,

MAY I ASK YOU a series of questions?
When you need someone, can I be that person?
When you are upset, can I be the one you turn to for your smile?
Can I be the first person you call when something happens good or bad in your day?
When you cry, can I be the one who dries away your tears?
And if all your answers are yes, follow suit when
I ask will you marry me today.

WITH LOVE,
    Your Future Husband